NORTH AMERICAN ROCKIES
CONIFEROUS FOREST

Wolf

Moose

Red Fox

Cottontail Rabbit

Marten

Grizzly Bear

Cockatiel

Scarlet Macaw

Toucan

Jaguar

NORTH AMERICA

EUROPE

ASIA

AFRICA

SOUTH AMERICA

AUSTRALIA

★AMAZON JUNGLE, BRAZIL
TROPICAL RAIN FOREST

Tapir

Sloth Bear

NORTH
AMERICA

EUROPE

ASIA

AFRICA

SOUTH
AMERICA

AUSTRALIA

★ EAST AFRICA
GRASSLAND AND SAVANNAH

Vulture

Rhinoceros Calf

Rhinoceros

Lion

Giraffe

Baby Giraffe

AFRICAN WATERING HOLE

African Elephant

Wildebeest

Termite Mound

Impala

Zebra

Baboon

Crocodile

Emu

Spiny Anteater

AUSTRALIAN DESERT

NORTH
AMERICA

EUROPE

ASIA

AFRICA

SOUTH
AMERICA

AUSTRALIA

" ★ CENTRAL AUSTRALIA
■ DESERT

Dingo

Red Kangaroo & Joey

Mulgara

Thorny Devil

NORTH
AMERICA
EUROPE
ASIA
AFRICA
SOUTH
AMERICA
AUSTRALIA

★ NORTH CENTRAL INDIA
■ DRY TROPICAL FOREST

Frilled Lizard

Blackbuck

Rhesus Monkey & Baby

Rhesus
Monkey

Cobra

ASIAN DRY TROPICAL FOREST